Table of Contents

INTRODUCTION

"We like to think that executives will hit the ground running and try to schedule a full day of meetings on their first day." -- quote from an SES Executive Onboarding Forum participant

On May 26, 2010, the Office of Personnel Management (OPM) partnered with the Senior Executives Association (SEA) and the Partnership for Public Service (PPS) to host an event where 115 individuals – including expert consultants, experienced and newer Senior Executive Service (SES) members, and executive resources (ER) and training professionals – gathered to discuss the importance of, and challenges to, onboarding Federal senior executives. During the event, experts presented their existing executive onboarding programs, and SES members shared their experiences and recommendations. Participants spent the second half of the day identifying components of an effective executive onboarding program.

As a result of this collaborative effort, OPM has developed this manual as a tool to assist agencies in creating an executive onboarding program and a business case for it. This document contains the end product of this 1-day event: an executive onboarding framework with information on the steps that are critical to developing and implementing a successful formal executive onboarding program from pre-boarding through the first year.

What is Executive Onboarding?

"I had to ask where my office was… There was a nametag on my door, but the office had an antiquated computer and no Blackberry." - quote from an SES Executive Onboarding Forum participant

Executive onboarding refers to the acquiring, accommodating, assimilating and accelerating of new leaders into the organizational culture and business.[1] The best onboarding strategies provide a fast track to meaningful, productive work and strong employee relationships.[2] Onboarding programs need to be tailored specifically to the needs of the organization and individuals. Executive onboarding should be strategic, so that it not only prevents executive derailment, but also expedites the executive's contribution to optimizing strategic achievement. In 2008, the Partnership for Public Service (PPS) and Booz Allen Hamilton conducted a study entitled *Getting On Board: A Model for Integrating and Engaging New Employees*. The study concluded that the successful onboarding of employees during their first year of service increases engagement, raises retention by as much as 25 percent, improves performance, and hastens the time to full productivity. In another study entitled *Unrealized Vision: Reimagining the Senior Executive Service* (August, 2009), PPS recommended OPM take the lead on creating an executive onboarding program for the Federal Government. This recommendation and the results from OPM's *2008 Senior Executive Survey* were the catalyst for the creation of this manual and the Governmentwide executive onboarding framework.

---

[1] http://www.cronos.dk/upload/File/Inspirationsmateriale/Onboarding%20Book%20Executive%20Summary.pdf
[2] http://www.cashnet.org/meetings/2007_Workshops/Fall07Handouts/OCDEOnboardingCASHHandout.pdf

THE BUSINESS CASE FOR EXECUTIVE ONBOARDING

"It is surprising how quickly you need to make decisions that are going to stick . . . and once you have made the decision, you are locked. It has to be really good the first time."
–quote from SEA/RHR focus group participant

Initially, agencies must be able to make the business case for developing the onboarding process, for example, by demonstrating and communicating success stories. Therefore, agencies should strategically target the area of greatest need and build a pilot process tailored to that need. Agencies should then define ways to measure success and assign accountable champions to drive positive outcomes. Agencies should also build and manage realistic expectations for early success.

Defining the Problem
"What I want to know is what the things that are going to surprise me are. I want to hit the ground running." –quote from SEA/RHR focus group participant

Much has been made of the impending "retirement tsunami," particularly in the senior leadership ranks in the Federal sector, where about 70 percent are eligible to retire in the near future.[3] This potential exodus has many implications for Federal agencies, including the need to integrate new leaders into organizations quickly. Within the Federal Government from January 2006 to the present day, 16 percent of SES members failed to complete their initial 1-year probationary period successfully, for reasons that included termination for performance, performance significantly below expectations, or voluntary resignation from the new position. According to the Corporate Leadership Council, new executives generally "fail" for five main reasons:

- ❖ They fail to establish a cultural fit;
- ❖ They fail to build teamwork with staff and peers;
- ❖ They are unclear about the performance expected of them;
- ❖ They lack political savvy; and
- ❖ Their organizations do not have a strategic, formal process to assimilate executives into the organization. [4]

Documented examples show that the effective onboarding of executives minimizes the need for terminations and costly replacements, by helping newly placed executives navigate the areas most critical to their success.[5] In light of the current hiring challenges, high-performing organizations use effective onboarding strategies to assimilate their leaders strategically; they do not apply a "sink or swim" mentality to new executives. Instead, these organizations understand they must provide support systems for new executives. [6] The most successful organizations understand they may choose to invest

---

[3] http://www.opm.gov/ses/executive_development/GettingXintoSES.pdf
[4] http://www.fmpconsulting.com/news_files/Spotlight%20on%20Executive%20Onboarding.pdf
[5] http://files.e2ma.net/10245/assets/docs/onboarding.pdf
[6] http://www.psychologytoday.com/blog/wired-success/201005/ceo-failures-how-boarding-can-help

valuable time and money positioning their executives to succeed rather than expending those same resources in lost productivity and turnover.

The Current State of Executive Onboarding in the Federal Government

Organization's Mistake
"We have hired a senior person. She should be able to figure it out."

Executive's Mistake
"I am a smart person. I need to prove myself and make my mark as soon as possible."

While many Federal agencies have established comprehensive onboarding programs for their employees, few agencies have implemented an onboarding process specifically geared toward assimilating and acculturating executives. Instead, agencies treat executive onboarding as a crude extension of employee orientation or with the nonchalant expectation that the executive will "figure it out." Some agencies do not emphasize the onboarding of new executives because they wish to avoid insulting established professionals, who may perceive an executive onboarding program as suggesting they require additional assistance. In fact, research indicates the onboarding of executives often is even more critical because of the significantly greater performance expectations executives face and the greater impact they have on the overall performance of the organization. Only a few agencies have implemented successful onboarding programs, including the National Science Foundation's New Executive Transition (NExT) Program and the executive onboarding programs within the Department of the Navy and the Department of Treasury's Office of the Comptroller of the Currency.

Because OPM recognizes the value of the ongoing assimilation of executives and other employees into Federal agencies, OPM has included a year-long orientation process among the five components of its new *End-to-End (E2E) Hiring Roadmap*. Though not specifically geared toward leadership positions, the *E2E Hiring Roadmap* can be used to help ensure Federal agencies recruit and retain the top talent they need to meet the complex challenges of the 21st century.

Additionally, OPM coordinates with the White House to conduct periodic 2-day executive orientations (i.e., SES briefings) for new SES members and equivalents. During these orientation sessions, participants learn about the President's agenda, vision, and values, and discuss the unique challenges they may face with their new leadership responsibilities. OPM has also partnered with the White House Offices of Presidential Personnel and Cabinet Affairs to create the President's Appointee Leadership Program (PALP) -- a 1-day program for noncareer SES and for Schedule C appointees, which cascades down from a leadership program at the Cabinet Secretary level. The main focus of this orientation program for political appointees is to establish the alignment between the administration and executives. Agencies are encouraged to use the SES orientation sessions and the PALP as an integral part of an executive onboarding program.

Agencies should also consider the need to develop onboarding solutions that address three types of newer SES members:

- Those who have grown within the agency;
- Those from outside the agency (but still within Government); and
- External hires from outside the Federal Government.

ONBOARDING DIVERSE EXECUTIVES

"It was very helpful to me to participate in the organization's diversity council where I met other women SES." - quote from an SES Executive Onboarding Forum participant

A successful onboarding process leads to an inclusive workplace, maximizing the talents of each person to achieve the vision and mission of the organization. Minority leaders and professionals often face particular challenges in integrating into a new organization, demonstrating their worth, and finding internal role models and mentors; therefore, effective onboarding is particularly important for this group[7]. Frequently, companies go to great lengths to acquire quality talent, only to unfortunately see many of their minority recruits depart within the first year. Consequently, onboarding programs should include cultural awareness and other diversity management priorities.

Cultural Awareness

Although agencies have traditionally devoted great effort to hiring diverse individuals into the SES, historically, little consideration has been given to the value of the diverse onboarding of new executives. Research indicates, however, that different individuals have different needs and different ways of processing information[8]; consequently, agencies should provide flexible onboarding programs that appropriately meet the needs of a diverse array of individuals. For example, agencies may consider providing diverse types of information or the same information in different ways, all tailored to the specific individual employee. Some agencies have achieved success by providing new executives access to a diverse pool of peer mentors with a variety of backgrounds, experience, and skills. Agencies have also hosted educational events, involving panels composed of diverse executives, to share advice on organizational transition and success for new executives.[9] The following are some additional diversity management and inclusion strategies for successful onboarding: treat similarly all similarly-situated individuals, and do not draw distinctions based upon non-merit factors (e.g., race, gender, age, ethnicity, disability, sexual orientation, gender identity, or religion); recognize and communicate the value of diversity and inclusion; provide training on equal employment opportunity and diversity management; and foster development of networks across the organization through shared and collaborative events and activities. [10]

---

[7] http://www.labmanager.com/articles.asp?ID=307

[8] http://www.ere.net/2008/11/17/onboarding-program-killers-15-common-errors-to-avoid/

[9] http://onboardingmargin.com/2010/11/integrating-diversity-inclusion-initiatives-with-new-hire-onboarding-programs/

[10] http://www.gcpartnership.com/Economic-Inclusion/Commission/~/media/Files/Inclusion/McCorvey_onboarding-socialization.ashx

Political Appointees

Agencies may apply the steps of the Executive Onboarding Framework contained in this manual to assist all types of executives in their transition into new organizations; however, agencies should bear in mind special considerations for political appointees. In September 2008, the National Academy of Public Administration, the Partnership for Public Service, and the University of Pennsylvania's Fels Institute published the results of a study entitled *Speeding up the Learning Curve: Observations from a Survey of Seasoned Political Appointees*. This study surveyed a group of Senate-confirmed appointees of former President George W. Bush, some of whom had performed substantial public service prior to their political appointments. The appointees shared their onboarding observations and experiences.

Survey respondents noted six key observations, for which agencies should provide education and support during the onboarding phase:

- **Knowledge of ethical standards and financial disclosure rules is necessary for rapid effectiveness.** This was true during the confirmation process, but was considered especially important during early months in office.

- **Performance and results matter.** Survey respondents said they thought two dimensions of performance were important or very important: measuring organizational results, and evaluating employee performance. Respondents emphasized the importance of leaders setting standards of performance and measuring progress against those standards, over the importance of managing financial, contract, or pay and benefits issues. Additionally, respondents focused on their need to understand expectations for their performance clearly and to receive direction on how their performance would be measured.

- **Policy development and implementation depend on understanding key Federal Government processes**. Respondents specifically identified four important factors: (1) understanding the President's priorities; (2) understanding how the executive branch operates; (3) understanding the budget process; and (4) mastering the process for policy development.

- **Relationships matter**. Respondents rated highly the importance of positive relationships with the U.S. Office of Management and Budget, career employees, and Congress.

- **Leadership, negotiation, and communication are key competencies**. All respondents cited leadership as a critical competency, followed closely by negotiation skills and communication.

- **Support of career executives is critical**. Respondents indicated their success depended heavily on three essential elements provided by career executives: (1)

knowledge of the agency's policies and processes; (2) support for the goals of agency political leaders; and (3) an understanding of the agency's internal culture. [11]

External Hires

Executives hired from outside the Federal Government are typically valued for their new skills and different perspectives, as well as their willingness to implement change[12]; however, Federal agencies need to actively help these newly-hired executives transition into their new positions if they want to reap the benefits of external hiring. Research reveals that external executive hires that are not provided with this type of support are *more* likely to fail than insiders promoted to executive positions. Studies indicate the success of incoming executives largely depends on the following:

- Understanding the unique aspects of the organizational culture;
- Understanding the dynamics of the teams the executive is entering (whether as a leader or colleague); and
- The personality, knowledge and leadership skills of the incoming executive. [13]

Agencies may help new executives with the first two requirements by providing information and guidance on the culture and team dynamics of the organization. Agencies may accomplish the third element by conducting individual assessments of new executives to inform onboarding and developmental strategies that will help the new executives integrate more successfully into the new organization with a shorter transition period.

PROGRAM ADMINISTRATION AND IMPLEMENTATION

Managers and supervisors, along with human resources professionals, should answer some key planning questions before implementing an onboarding program or revamping a current orientation program.

What to Consider when Implementing an Onboarding Program:

- Is your onboarding program tied to a specific business need?
- Is there a need for multi-function collaboration?
- Is there a dynamic between career and political appointees that needs to be addressed?
- Do you have stakeholder support? Without it, your onboarding program will not work.

[11]http://transition2008.wordpress.com/2009/05/12/lessons-learned-past-political-appointees/
[12] http://jmo.e-contentmanagement.com/archives/vol/17/issue/2/article/3743/onboarding-externally-hired-executives
[13] http://managementhelp.org/blogs/leadership/2010/11/10/executive-onboarding/

- What are the key relationships that are going to make or break a successful transition for a new SES member?
- How will you obtain commitment from upper management?

When developing and implementing an executive onboarding program, consider the following tips:

Secure program commitment from senior leadership

Program success depends upon senior leadership commitment, participation, and support from the highest levels, to provide buy-in and encouragement for new executives to complete the onboarding program successfully.

Establish relevant program objectives

Agencies must initially develop program objectives, informed by the identification of key issues concerning the relevant onboarding population. At a minimum, the onboarding program should assist new executives in understanding the organization's business and culture, help clarify performance expectations, and shorten the executives' learning curve to enable them to perform to their full potential as quickly as possible. For example, relevant onboarding program objectives may include the following:

- Enabling successful transitions for executives hired from outside the Federal Government;
- Developing executives' awareness of the agency's mission, culture, people, and business processes; and
- Promoting the value and understanding of diversity management and inclusion.

Target core leadership competencies

Agencies should consider the following four key core leadership competencies:

- Understanding the organization, key stakeholders, business goals and objectives;
- Understanding the organization's culture, including its unwritten rules;
- Navigating internal networks and relationships; and
- Understanding the organization's expectations for executive leadership.

Use a blended learning approach

Agencies may most effectively provide new executives with the tools, information, skill-enhancement, and support through multiple and diverse mechanisms. To help new executives reach their full performance as quickly as possible, agencies should provide various learning options to reinforce messages (e.g., a dedicated website for executives, handbook, online tutorials, peer mentoring and executive coaching). Agencies should deliver important information through a variety of ways and at several different points throughout the onboarding period (e.g., before arrival, during the first month, 3-to-6-

month follow-up), helping executives stay engaged and focused on learning throughout their onboarding period. Agencies should facilitate networking and relationship-building by providing information on, and interactions with, cross-agency organizations and employees. For example, some organizations pre-schedule one-on-one meetings between the new executive and key organizational contacts during the executive's first 30 days. Agencies may also offer informal meet-and-greet gatherings to bring leaders together to network and share information.

Frame the program in terms of hours

When onboarding executives, agencies should clearly and specifically articulate the time frames for executives to complete the required tasks, allowing the executives to more effectively plan and schedule time to complete the tasks. In typical onboarding programs, executives are assigned tasks to be completed at various points during the onboarding stage (e.g., the first week, the first 30 days, 60 days, 90 days and, finally, the first year). Ideally, the new executive's manager will provide the executive with a calendar already populated with onboarding tasks, as well as other essential meetings and activities, to help the new executive structure his or her schedule and time.

Establish clear accountability mechanisms

Agencies should define and clearly communicate to new executives how the executives will be held accountable for completing the onboarding program in order to ensure effective participation. Agencies may include the executive's supervisor as a key facilitator in the onboarding and long-term integration process to bolster accountability by ensuring the new executive's onboarding needs are being addressed and by monitoring performance.

Establish program metrics and evaluation criteria

Onboarding programs should ultimately have a positive impact on both individual and organizational performance; therefore, agencies should identify and establish meaningful evaluation criteria to measure program success. The establishment of meaningful metrics (e.g., retention rates, performance ratings, and organizational performance measures) helps to ensure that an agency's onboarding program is aligned with the agency's larger strategic goals. Agencies should also conduct regular evaluations to monitor program success and identify necessary adjustments to the program's design and delivery.

Keep the new executive's family in mind

Agencies may readily enhance the effectiveness of onboarding programs by considering how to support work/life issues, including how the onboarding programs may help the families of new executives adjust to a new job, particularly where the job required relocation. [14]

---

[14] http://www.fmpconsulting.com/news_files/Spotlight%20on%20Executive%20Onboarding.pdf

Executive Onboarding Program Derailers

The following are several common omissions or obstacles to successful onboarding programs:

- **No written plan**. Successful onboarding programs begin with the development of a formal written plan, integrated into agencies' overall business plans, and aligned with succession, talent management, and recruitment plans.
- **Ownership by Human Resources (HR)**. The onboarding program design should make it clear that onboarding effectiveness depends on commitment and buy-in from the top of the organization, and sharing this commitment throughout the organization, including by hiring and supervising officials.
- **No continuous improvement component**. The best onboarding programs have a formal process for continuously identifying and assessing successes and deficiencies, to inform improvements.
- **No best practice sharing**. Onboarding programs must have a formal design component for the rapid identification, adoption, and sharing of best practices related to onboarding.
- **No data-based decision-making**. Agencies should make major onboarding program design and resource decisions based primarily on data, rather than anecdotal understanding or historical practice.
- **Delays in offering onboarding**. Agencies frequently postpone most onboarding components until a large group of new hires can participate in a single session; however, delays hinder new-hire productivity and increase the risk of new-hire mistakes or failure. Agencies may improve timely delivery of onboarding by providing services on multiple occasions or by requiring onboarding to be conducted no later than the first week after a new employee is hired. [15]

Views from New Senior Executives

During the onboarding panel discussion hosted by OPM, the Partnership for Public Service, and Senior Executives Association, new executives offered their perspectives and onboarding experiences within their agencies, highlighting the benefit of consulting current SES members when developing or modifying agency executive onboarding programs. The following are examples of some of their comments:

What were the biggest challenges to being a new SES?

- Family issues provided a disincentive for accepting SES jobs (e.g., personal transitions, living away from family).
- Going to an agency where the new executive did not know anyone.
- The deputy in the office had applied for the SES position and had expected to be selected.

---

[15] http://www.hrnetworkgroup.com.au/newsletter/issue29.html

- Inheriting a budget crisis without any knowledge of causality or solution; being held responsible for all mistakes or failures in the agency.

- Transition from the role of peer to supervisor.

- Difficulty in establishing credibility and qualifications.

- Predecessor had a different style.

- Difficult to establish and improve relationships successfully.

What tools were useful to meet those challenges?

- Interactions with the Secretary and major division heads provided a good learning experience and opportunity to meet people

- Predecessor stayed on for 60 days to provide guidance, and upon departure, other managers were very supportive.

- Familiarity with the program and opportunity to select a deputy.

Knowing what you know now, what would you have done differently during transition?

- Address earlier staff preferences for past practices.

- Obtain more information on congressional relations, including identity of key committee members, sources of information, and priorities.

What recommendations do you have to improve executive onboarding?

- Continuous engagement is important for new executives to learn their new agencies.

- Agencies should give senior executives "permission" to take time to ask questions and learn the organization.

- New executives can establish credibility by being included in networking and collaborative activities with established executives.

- Agencies should provide photographs and names of key agency officials.

- Agencies should inform new executives of training requirements, and provide a position description, objectives, performance standards, and an action checklist before reporting on the first day.

- Agencies should consider onboarding a mission-critical program and properly provide leadership support and funding.

- Agencies should administer 360° assessments to all new executives.

- Agencies should help new executives obtain agency-wide perspective by supporting their participation in cross-agency events.

PROVEN TECHNIQUES & BEST PRACTICES IN EXECUTIVE ONBOARDING

Private-Sector Organizations

Many private-sector organizations have successful executive onboarding programs. OPM invited one such organization, PepsiCo, to share information about its executive onboarding. Phil Golino, Director of Leadership Development at PepsiCo, and Marjorie Derven of Hudson Research Consulting shared program information and results of PepsiCo's onboarding program. In short, PepsiCo identified a significant difference in satisfaction and performance between managers who went through the onboarding program and those who did not attend the onboarding program, with those participating in the program reporting far greater levels of satisfaction while demonstrating higher performance. Furthermore, PepsiCo selected 90 percent of its General Managers from within the organization. PepsiCo provided the following summary of some of its successful onboarding practices.

PepsiCo's Onboarding Process for General Managers:

Information for Candidates and New Hires:
- Provide relevant information to candidates on the terms and conditions of their prospective employment (e.g., candidly discuss with candidates the need for relocation in order to achieve career advancement);
- Provide regular opportunities for new hires to familiarize themselves with the workplace, and create an environment conducive for new hires to ask questions and seek information; and
- Provide new hires, from the first day of employment, with information and opportunities to build important workplace relationships.

Design, Development and Deployment Methodology:
- Develop onboarding solutions linked with specific business needs;
- Identify key colleagues and stakeholders with whom new hires should immediately establish positive relationships;
- Create functional checklists to standardize the onboarding process;
- Create and maintain a business dashboard to allow executives to maintain operational awareness while maintaining a strategic focus;
- Provide executives a list of agency contacts, identifying the key 5-7 people with whom executives most interact, including subject-matter experts; and
- At the outset, develop and apply performance appraisal metrics that may be integrated into an organizational assessment tool, enabling new leaders to align individual performance with organizational goals.

Create a Business Assessment Tool:
- Create a list of 90 questions for executives to use during their first 90 days. Executives use this set of strategic questions as a roadmap during their first 90 days. They seek answers to these questions to better understand the office, the

agency, and their role in contributing to the organization. Executives use the results of this exercise to develop an action plan by the 90-day mark, which serves as a foundation for discussing the way forward with senior leadership.

- Require managers to bring the answers to the 90 questions with them to an event for all new executives. (Army has developed a similar structure for helping commanders pinpoint the existing problems in the organization; they conducted interviews with the staff to identify blind spots).

The following private-sector companies also apply additional successful executive onboarding practices:

Johnson & Johnson, Canada

Johnson & Johnson tailors its onboarding program to the specific needs of each new employee. For example, new hires from outside the company enter a different onboarding track than those hired from within the company. Internal hires are also onboarded differently according to their key skill gaps, which the company has previously identified through its performance management process. Johnson & Johnson's onboarding program also includes the following:

- An external onboarding coach who provides support to the new executive for 6 months, including by collecting and using business/organizational data (e.g., employee survey feedback, customer feedback) anonymously to prepare an onboarding development charter for the new employee. The business/organizational data is put into an individualized dashboard and provides a stakeholder relationship map;
- A senior mentor 'buddy' outside direct reporting relationships, who helps acclimate the new employee to the organization and provides advice on policies, procedures, and the unwritten rules of the organization;
- Networking appointments with key leaders;
- Workshops to help new executives plan their onboarding process and network; and
- Solicitation of feedback on the onboarding progress at the 6-month milestone of employment to identify transition issues and adjustments.

American Express

- On the first day of employment, provide each new hire with an HR partner, hiring manager, and external assimilation coach to formulate a 100-day transition plan, and to provide continuous support during the onboarding stage;
- Build an Individual Development Plan (IDP) for each new executive based on individual assessment data collected during the recruitment stage, requirements of the specific job, and the executive's career aspirations;
- Facilitate formal networking meetings with the CEO and senior management team;

- Provide learning and networking experiences involving various parts of the company; and
- At 6-month milestone:
    - Provide executives with 360° assessment, and use this data for further development
    - Gather feedback to improve onboarding process
    - Provide for new executives' participation in annual New Leaders Orientation Summit

Bristol-Myers Squibb

- Assess leadership ability and organizational fit at the interview stage, which will help determine the executive's future development and where he or she will be most effective in the future;
- Schedule meetings for the new hire with influential colleagues;
- Track the progress of each new executive during the first year of employment; and
- Tailor onboarding process based on information gathered about the individual during the hiring process (e.g., information obtained during pre-selection assessments and behavioral interviews)

Technology for Onboarding Programs

Many high-performing, innovative organizations leverage technology to optimize their onboarding processes.[16] These organizations achieve more efficient methods, through technology, to convey data to new executives and to track their progress (e.g., through intranet portals and web-based tools). Additionally, these solutions allow organizations to provide information and onboarding services before the new executives' first day on the job. For example, Capital One designed a series of e-learning modules that new hires can access on a website. The site provides information on culture, values and business lines, and includes PDF versions of essential forms to download in advance of the on-site onboarding class. Such technology-aided preparation enables immediate and direct knowledge-sharing between managers and new executives, and helps new hires feel much more prepared and familiar with the company's policies when they begin their new employment.

The U.S. Government Accountability Office (GAO) uses an online system to notify appropriate organizational units in advance of the arrival of a new employee so appropriate personnel can prepare information technology (IT) equipment, establish IT system accounts, and prepare facilities and utilities.[17] Also, the U.S. Department of Agriculture uses automated processes that allow new hires to complete all necessary forms before the first day of work.

---

[16] http://www.silkroad.com/SiteGen/Uploads/Public/SRT/Whitepaper/OnboardingBenchmarchReport.pdf
[17] http://www.workforce.com/section/recruiting-staffing/feature/onboarding-greater-engagement/

Such uses of technology allow organizations to improve the speed and ease with which the organizations complete onboarding preparations and make it easier for new executives to access information and complete paperwork. Consequently, new executives will experience a much smoother and customer-friendly transition into the new organization, while having the support to concentrate on important responsibilities rather than transactional procedures.

Networking

Organizations also enhance the scope and success of their onboarding programs by including networking strategies during executives' transitions into their new organizations. For example, the Shell Oil Company invites new executives to an onboarding workshop 6 months into their new jobs, bringing together all new employees from around the world. At these events, new executives share experiences and solutions on goals, challenges, and expectations. In addition to providing an opportunity for knowledge transfer, these events provide opportunities to develop relationships, lines of communication, and future collaboration.

MEASURING SUCCESS

Organizations with effective onboarding programs are able to identify specific onboarding metrics tied to strategic organizational outcomes. These organizations have measured the impact of onboarding on their retention successes.[18] Organizations also examine important indicators such as expense savings, customer satisfaction (internal and external), processing time for employee equipment and tools, and employee engagement. Many tools can help assist in planning, documenting, and evaluating an onboarding program. One of these tools is the Logic Model. The logic model is an evaluation tool that will guide program planning, documentation, and reporting, as well as program implementation, monitoring, and evaluation. Agencies should complete logic models to determine the inputs, activities, target participants, and short, intermediate and long term goals of their executive onboarding programs.

EXECUTIVE ONBOARDING FRAMEWORK: KEY COMPONENTS

In order to develop and implement a successful onboarding program, Federal agencies must emphasize a number of key elements, and proper sequencing of these critical tasks will produce better results.[19] The following are key components to which every agency should give special prominence:

During the **first few days**, agencies should support new executives' emphasis on:
- Learning the protocols and processes of the agency
- Obtaining clarification of expectations
- Engaging in timely and accurate communication with key stakeholders

---

[18] http://www.silkroad.com/SiteGen/Uploads/Public/SRT/Whitepaper/OnboardingBenchmarchReport.pdf
[19] http://www.resourcesinaction.com/blog/ceo-on-boarding-question-2/

- Devising regular and effective communication processes with peers, superiors, and other stakeholders. *This process starts on the first day and improves on an ongoing basis.*

During the **first 30 days,** new executives should emphasize the following:
- Understanding cultural issues
- Obtaining consensus on top strategic priorities
- Devising a 90-day plan (see appendix for a list of strategic questions that can be used to develop an action plan)
- Familiarization with senior leadership relationships and determining potential risks and problem areas in the new environment
- Examining and considering improvements in the immediate organizational structure

During the **next 30 days,** the key tasks for a new executive typically include:
- Identifying early wins
- Identifying learning priorities
- Finalizing an action plan to discuss with senior leaders
- Refining specific job expectations and resource requirements with the executive's manager

During **days 60 to 90**, the new executive should emphasize:
- Articulating a vision and engaging the team
- Developing and implementing action plans to support execution of early wins
- Strengthening alliances with key stakeholders
- Maintaining regular and effective communication processes with peers, superiors, and other stakeholders.

CONCLUSION

On average, new executives require a minimum of 6 months to become fully productive in their role.[20] Federal agencies may readily pave the way to ensure a new executive's effective integration into their organizations by implementing a specialized executive onboarding program – one of the simplest and most cost-effective strategies to optimizing the success of new hires. Executive onboarding programs help prevent and address a number of important issues common to most new executives – making the transition for new executives smoother, more efficient, and more positive, and allowing new executives to transition quickly and effectively into their new roles. Successful onboarding further contributes to leadership retention, and promotes long-term organizational success.

---

[20] http://www.fmpconsulting.com/news_files/Spotlight%20on%20Executive%20Onboarding.pdf

APPENDIX A

SAMPLE STRATEGIC QUESTIONS

Below is a sample set of questions executives should ask and get answers for to better understand the agency and their role in contributing to the organization. The process of asking and ultimately answering these questions should enable the executive to quickly understand the organization and perform basic job functions; know the correct individuals or departments who can provide assistance and answer questions; perform job tasks in compliance with agency and Government policies; and access key information about leadership resources and development opportunities. *Note: The number of questions is not important, but the substance and relevance of the questions to the success of the executive is important.*

Questions leaders need to:

Ask themselves and/or their mentor	Ask other leaders	Ask manager and/or key stakeholders	Ask direct reports	Ask others in order to access information about available training resources
What is the agency vision and mission?	What are the 3 things we should be very proud of as an organization, and why?	Who are our customers?	What is a recent management decision you did not understand?	How can I advance in the organization?
How are my goals and objectives tied to the vision?	What are the unspoken norms?	Why do customers do business with us?	What does the leadership team do that gets in the way of you doing your job?	How do I request training?
What does the end state look like?	Where do the great ideas come from in your organization?	How and when have we made it hard for them to do business with us?	How can we communicate management decisions more effectively?	How do I register for training?
What is the state of the talent within my group?	How is personal success measured?	What do our customers need from us now?	How do you feel at the start of the workweek?	How and when can I initiate a leadership assessment process?
What are the organization norms regarding dress and appearance?	How do you encourage others to communicate the "core values"?	What will our customers need from us in the future?	How do you feel at the end of the workweek?	Which organizations provide professional development opportunities for

				SES members?
What are the organization norms regarding punctuality?	How do you help a new employee understand the culture of the organization?	What gets in the way of us doing our job?	What are the key metrics to track progress and success?	With whom should I discuss development opportunities?
What is the process for requesting and documenting leave?	When faced with two equally qualified candidates how do you determine whom to hire?	What are the expectations for my role as a leader?	What are the short term priorities?	How do I find out about required training?
Are there any quick wins?	How do I locate information about agency departments and offices?	How is departmental success measured?	What tools are used to manage schedules (appointments)- paper, outlook?	How can I access available leadership training resources?
What support do I need to achieve success for my organization?	What is one mistake you witness leaders making more frequently than others?	What are the organizational taboos?	What is my role in emergency evacuation?	Where can I find recommended reading materials?
Where can I go to find the most recent Employee Viewpoint Survey (or other employee opinion survey) results for my organization?	What is the one behavior or trait you have seen derail more leaders' careers?	What are some of the challenges that previous incumbents in this position have encountered?	Where is the alternate operating location?	When and where is the next SES Orientation Briefing? How do I register?
What is my role in COOP?	Why do people stay in this organization?	Where can I find information about the current administration's priorities?	What process is used to collect our customers' needs and measure their satisfaction?	Are there any organizational leadership tools I should be aware of?
What strategic relationships and internal networks should I be aware of?	What motivates senior management?	What key policies should I be aware of in the first month and which ones do I own?	What are the short term priorities for the organization and my office?	What are a few resources you would recommend to someone looking to gain insight into becoming a better leader?
What do I want to be remembered for?	What are the organizational norms about travel (not the GSA/official rules)?	Who are my key partners and what do they do/provide?	What are the results of the most recent third-party inspection (IG, GAO, etc.)?	What are you doing to ensure you continue to learn and grow as a leader?

What are the major risks associated with my position- to me, to my organization?	In my first twelve months, what can I do to help you and your staff be successful?	What are the results of the most recent employee morale survey?	What are 3 capabilities we have that are under-developed or under-utilized and what should we do about that?	What is one characteristic you believe every leader should possess?
How does the work I do contribute to the overall success of the organization?	Who are the "power players"?	What is the current and future year budget outlook?	What are the three things you would change around here and why?	What skills do I need to be most effective?
What is the organization's commitment to telework and other work-life programs?	What is one thing you would change about the organization?	Which congressional committees are concerned with the organization's mission and funding?	What is the most pressing issue for me to address with our customers?	When should I complete my Executive Development Plan (EDP)?

APPENDIX B

Executive Onboarding Program Framework for the Federal Government

Executive onboarding is a way of acquiring, accommodating, assimilating and accelerating new leaders into the organizational culture and business. Documented examples show that onboarding of leaders minimizes the chances of costly replacements and terminations by helping newly-placed executives navigate the areas that are most critical to success. The best approaches recognize that a successful onboarding process involves process owners, process champions and new executives. The following are typical responsibilities for each group:

Process Owners (e.g., Human Resources, Executive Resources)
- Serve as a bridge between the recruiting phase and the onboarding phase;
- Ensure appropriate feedback mechanisms are in place for all involved in the process;
- Assess the need for additional organizational support/resources (e.g., IT, facilities);
- Are prepared to address issues of diversity (diversity is a broader concept than ethnicity, race, gender and age; it also includes disability, religion, nationality, and sexual orientation); and
- Partner with the manager and executive to focus the executive's transition efforts in the most productive directions.

Process Champions (e.g., senior leaders, managers, supervisors, mentors, coaches)
- Provide explicit encouragement for new executives to take time to learn, build relationships, and set the stage for performance;
- Are accountable for seeing that the strategy and process are accomplished;
- Ensure expectations are clear and provide regular and constructive feedback;
- Consider diversity in all aspects of onboarding;
- Assist the new executive with integration into his or her peer group; and
- Explain and set realistic milestones and cultural expectations (e.g., decisions that can be made without manager approval, communication styles).

New Executives
- Actively learn about the organization's history, values, vision and mission, strategic plans, leadership structure, metrics and performance, processes and practices;
- Take responsibility for ensuring integration is accomplished effectively by achieving the measurements for success that have been put in place, absorbing critical information, and building valuable relationships; and
- Regularly communicate expectations, objectives, and accomplishments.

The following framework is intended to be general enough to meet the majority of the needs of all new and newly-assigned executives from pre-boarding through the first year; however, agencies should modify the framework and assign responsibility according to unique agency processes and practices and according to each new executive's individual needs. Agencies should assign responsibility for these tasks to specific offices and individuals to ensure accountability.

Tasks outlined in the framework may be accomplished in several ways, including handbooks, webinars, agency websites, face-to-face meetings, checklists, handouts, retreats, e-binders, transition meetings, etc. We also recommend agencies specify the amount of time it should typically take (in hours) for the executive to accomplish the tasks within each phase. Also, see in the framework where automation is recommended ( ).

PRE-BOARD
The goal of the pre-boarding phase is to plan and prepare for the executive's arrival and to ensure the executive's successful entrance into the organization.

☐   Provide the executive with:
     o Bios and resumes of direct reports
     o Required applications and forms (e.g., benefits, ethics information, travel card application)
(Encourage the executive to review and complete necessary paperwork before the first employment day.)

☐   Work with security to ensure timely clearance processing.
☐   Work with IT and Facilities to coordinate work space so the executive has an appropriate parking space, office, equipment, identification, PDA/Blackberry, etc.
☐   Order nameplates, flags and business cards.
☐   Pre-populate the executive's calendar with tasks in the framework as well as other essential activities and training. This will demonstrate leadership support for the strategic onboarding of the executive as well as help ensure the executive takes the necessary time to complete the specific tasks (e.g., meetings with mentor/sponsor/coach, lunch with senior leaders, formal feedback sessions).
☐   Create a list of key stakeholders and agency leaders with name, title, phone number and email address. Provide to the executive on the first day.
☐   Assign an executive sponsor. A sponsor accelerates the new executive's ability to quickly address and properly deal with early confusing issues. Questions about "normal protocol" in the organization, finding the right people to go to for information, correct procedures, and learning what is "right" and "wrong" should be easily answered by a sponsor. Be sure the sponsor knows his or her responsibilities. Provide a checklist if possible.
☐   Assign a mentor to help immerse the executive into the culture of the organization.
☐   Assign a coach to help the executive progress in his or her current position, as well as with individual development and career goals.

- ☐ 🖳 Develop a briefing book or website with:
  - ○ Key information about the agency (e.g., structure and mission, background, financial information)
  - ○ Organizational chart and phone book
  - ○ Photos and bios of key executives
  - ○ List of acronyms
  - ○ Message from the Director/Head of Agency
  - ○ Benefits, work life programs, transit subsidy information
  - ○ Required training information
  - ○ List of recurring meetings
  - ○ Maps and building information
  - ○ Payroll calendar
  - ○ Information of personal interest (e.g., information packet on local schools and realtors)

- ☐ 🖳 Obtain items with the agency logo or brand to give on the first day as welcome gifts – a nice touch to say we are glad you are here and you are a part of our team.

- ☐ 🖳 Schedule mandatory training (e.g., IT security, ethics, No Fear Act, performance management, employee and labor relations, Hatch Act, EEO, diversity awareness).

- ☐ 🖳 Executive should provide direct reports and staff with a bio, photo and a letter of introduction.

DAY 1/WEEK 1

The goal of the first day is to ensure the executive is welcomed into the organization by senior leadership and new staff and is satisfactorily in-processed. The remainder of the week should be dedicated to deliberate introduction and acclimation of the executive into the organization as well as training to help the executive understand pitfalls and critical issues.

- ☐ Welcome the executive by conducting a swearing-in ceremony, including the executive's family, photo and a press release.

- ☐ Introduce the executive to direct reports, staff, senior leaders, etc.

- ☐ Produce an article for agency publication to note the arrival of the executive.

- ☐ Executive should complete any paperwork and security requirements that were not completed during the pre-boarding phase.

- ☐ Conduct an executive briefing, transition meeting or other forum to provide the executive with information about the work group. The briefing should include:
  - ○ The 12-month calendar and a letter from the previous executive to gain a perspective on organizational history, culture, priorities and "lessons learned"
  - ○ Fact sheets on the "hot issues" that will require the executive's attention within the first 90 days
  - ○ A quick introduction to personnel policies and rules (financial "dos and don'ts", acquisitions, hiring, firing, contractor support)
  - ○ A discussion of initial projects and roles and responsibilities, including

	past performance standards o Training and information designed to provide initial familiarity with crucial systems and procedures. These are crash courses but will serve their purpose by making executives aware immediately of vital systems, laws, procedures, etc.
❐	Introduce the executive to his or her assigned mentor and sponsor.
❐	Executive should review the list of key contacts and stakeholders and begin to schedule introductory calls/meetings.
❐	Meet with executive to ensure job roles and responsibilities are clearly communicated.
❐	Take the executive to lunch.
❐	Executive should meet with direct reports and staff.
❐	Executive should attend any necessary training as described in the pre-boarding phase.
❐	Executive should create an action plan. This can take the form of a set of strategic questions an executive should ask and get the answers to over time, in order to better understand the agency and his or her role in contributing to the organization. (See Appendix A of the OPM manual "Hit The Ground Running: Establishing a Model Executive Onboarding Program" for a list of sample strategic questions.)
❐	Register for the OPM SES Briefing for New Executives https://www.leadership.opm.gov/planning/sesbriefings/index.aspx.
❐	Provide the executive with the resources, tools and time to successfully accomplish tasks in this phase.

FIRST 30 DAYS

The goal within the first 30 days is to establish roles and responsibilities of the new executive as they relate to performance, development and ethical behavior. Executives should also begin to build relationships and business partnerships.

❐	Finalize the executive's performance objectives.
❐	Executive should create an Executive Development Plan (EDP) with his or her manager and solicit input from coach/mentor.
❐	Executive should schedule a formal feedback session with his or her manager and coach/mentor.
❐	Facilitate networking opportunities and provide resources to make networking possible.
❐	Discuss with the executive his or her individual work styles and preferences.
❐	Executive should meet with his or her coach.
❐	Executive should seek out unwritten rules (e.g., how to get things done; who can help and who can't or won't; what to do and, more importantly, what not to do) with mentor, sponsor and peers—this could be included in the risk assessment initiated in week 1.
❐	Executive should begin scheduling appointments with key stakeholders from other

organizations (e.g., programs, policies, and budget). Executive should consult with his or her manager or mentor to identify stakeholders.
❒ Provide the executive with the resources, tools and time to successfully accomplish tasks in this phase.
❒ 💻 Contact the executive to get feedback on his or her experience after 30 days.

FIRST 90 DAYS

The goal within the first 90 days is to cultivate the new executive by building competence in the job and providing frequent opportunities for open forum discussions. Executives should begin to have a full workload while managers monitor performance and provide early feedback.

❒ 💻 Executive should identify professional development opportunities.
❒ Executive should develop an action plan based on answers to the strategic questions provided in Week 1.
❒ Executive should review performance objectives with his or her manager.
❒ Provide the executive with the resources, tools and time to successfully accomplish tasks in this phase.
❒ 💻 Contact the executive to get feedback on his or her experience after 90 days.

6 TO 9 MONTHS

The goal within the first 6 months is to provide guidance and feedback to the executive to ensure continued success and to make plans for his or her future with the organization.

❒ Executive should engage in a leadership assessment process (e.g., 360, Myers-Briggs Type Indicator) for developmental purposes and to identify areas for improvement; follow up with coaching and/or an action plan if appropriate.
❒ 💻 Executive should schedule a formal feedback session with his or her manager.
❒ Executive should reflect on his or her role with coach/mentor.
❒ 💻 Executive should revisit the EDP to assess professional development goals and track progress.
❒ Provide the executive with the resources, tools and time to successfully accomplish tasks in this phase.
❒ 💻 Contact the executive to get feedback on his or her experience after 6 months.
❒ 💻 Notify the Hiring Manager the probationary period is ending.

1 YEAR

The goal within the first year is to monitor performance, individual development, goals and desires and to engage the executive in advancing the mission of the organization.

☐	Executive should complete a 360° assessment (or other leadership assessment process) in addition to the annual performance appraisal.
☐	Executive should develop a roadmap for long-term success.
☐	Provide an anniversary pin and card from the Secretary/Director.
☐	Follow up to ensure executive has attended the OPM SES Briefing.
☐	Provide the executive with the resources, tools and time to successfully accomplish tasks in this phase.
☐	Contact the executive to get feedback on his or her experience after 1 year.
☐	Close out and assess next steps.

The onboarding process may conclude 1 year after the incoming executive's arrival, with a final 360° assessment or other leadership review. This provides the leader with additional feedback and an opportunity to see if change efforts are working as intended.

The following chart provides an overview of **Key Onboarding Goals**. While all executives are expected to continually learn, build relationships, deliver results and constantly monitor performance and individual development, the time periods identified in this chart simply illustrate when those objectives should be emphasized during the onboarding process.

Goals	Pre-Boarding	Day 1/ Week 1	30 Days	90 Days	6 Months	1 Year
1. Plan and prepare for the executive's arrival and ensure the executive's successful entrance into the organization	→→→→→→→→					
2. Ensure the executive is welcomed into the organization by senior leadership and new staff and is satisfactorily in-processed. The remainder of the week should be dedicated to deliberate introduction and acclimation of the executive into the organization as well as training to help the executive understand pitfalls and critical issues.		→→→→→→				
3. Establish roles and responsibilities of the new executive as they relate to performance, development and ethical behavior. Executives should also begin to build relationships and business partnerships.		→→→→→→→				
4. Cultivate the new executive by building competence in the job and providing frequent opportunities for open forum discussions. Executives should begin to have a full workload while managers monitor performance and provide early feedback.		→→→→→→→→→→→				
5. Provide guidance and feedback to the executive to ensure continued success and to make plans for his or her future with the organization.				→→→→→→→→→→→→		
6. Monitor performance, individual development, goals and desires and engage the executive in advancing the mission of the organization.					→→→→→→→	

www.ingramcontent.com/pod-product-compliance
Lightning Source LLC
Chambersburg PA
CBHW081419170526
45166CB00010B/3405